Tough Topics

New Brothers and Sisters

Elizabeth Raum

Heinemann Library
Chicago, Illinois

© 2008 Heinemann Library
a division of Reed Elsevier Inc.
Chicago, Illinois

Customer Service 888-454-2279

Visit our website at www.heinemannlibrary.com

Designed by Joanna Hinton-Malivoire
Photo research by Tracy Cummins and Heather Mauldin
Printed in China by South China Printing.

12 11 10 09 08
10 9 8 7 6 5 4 3 2 1

Library of Congress Cataloging-in-Publication Data
Raum, Elizabeth.
  New brothers and sisters / Elizabeth Raum.
      p. cm. -- (Tough topics)
  Includes bibliographical references and index.
  ISBN-13: 978-1-4329-0820-1 (hc), ISBN-10: 1-4329-0820-0 (hc)
  ISBN-13: 978-1-4329-0825-6 (pb), ISBN-10: 1-4329-0825-1 (pb)
  1. Newborn infants--Juvenile literature. 2. Brothers and sisters--Juvenile literature. 3. Parent and child--Juvenile literature. I. Title.
  HQ774.R38 2008
  306.875--dc22

                                    2007034262

Acknowledgments
The author and publisher are grateful to the following for permission to reproduce copyright material:
©Corbis pp. **10** (Norbert Schaefer), **14** (James Noble), **15** (Blend Images/Ariel Skelley), **19** (Jose Luis Pelaez, Inc.), **24** (zefa/Larry Williams), **27** (Randy Faris), **28** (Don Mason); ©Getty Images pp. **4** (Jack Hollingsworth), **5** (Ciaran Griffin), **6** (Anne Ackermann), **7** (Alexander Walter), **8** (Zia Soleil), **9** (Marc Romanelli), **12** (Terry Vine), **13** (Tetra Images), **16** (Barbara Peacock), **17** (Marcus Mok), **18** (Ghislain & Marie David), **20** (Royalty Free), **21** (Spyros Bourboulis), **22** (Simon Watson), **23** (Trish Gant), **25** (Ellen Denuto), **26** (Ryan McVay), **29** (Anne Ackermann); ©Shutterstock p. **11** (Rohit Seth).

Cover photograph reproduced with permission of ©Corbis/Patrik Giardino.

Every effort has been made to contact copyright holders of any material reproduced in this book. Any omissions will be rectified in subsequent printings if notice is given to the publisher.

The author would like to thank Ms. Helen Scully, Guidance Counselor, Central Elementary School, Warren Township, New Jersey, for her valuable assistance.

Contents

Some words are shown in bold, **like this**. You can find out what they mean by looking in the Glossary.

A New Baby

Families come in different sizes. Some are small. Some are big. Some are still growing.

▲This large family is having fun together.

◄ Some children are surprised when their parents tell them that a new brother or sister will join the family.

Families grow when a new baby is born or when parents **adopt** a child. Some children are happy to learn that the family is growing. Others worry about the changes that a new brother or sister will bring.

Why Do We Have to Wait so Long?

◄ The baby grows bigger every day making your mom's belly grow, too.

It takes nine months for a baby to grow big enough to be born. If parents **adopt** a child, that takes time, too. Many families use this time to get ready for the new baby.

Being **pregnant** may make your mom tired. You can be a big help. You can practice being a big sister or brother by helping around the house.

How to Help Out

- Fold clothes

- Set or clear table

- Pick up toys

- Get things for your mom

- Sweep the floor

- Play quietly by yourself

◄This girl helps paint her new brother's or sister's room.

You can help prepare a place for the baby. You may help make room for the crib and shop for new clothes and baby supplies. You might sort through your own baby toys and set some aside for your new brother or sister.

You might enjoy learning about what you were like as a baby. How big were you? How did you act? Learning about what you were like as a baby is a good way to learn what to expect from a new brother or sister.

▼Look through your baby photos with a parent.

What Will the Baby Be Like?

Newborn babies are tiny and helpless. They cannot even hold up their own heads. They must be lifted very carefully.

▼This newborn baby fits easily into an adult's hands.

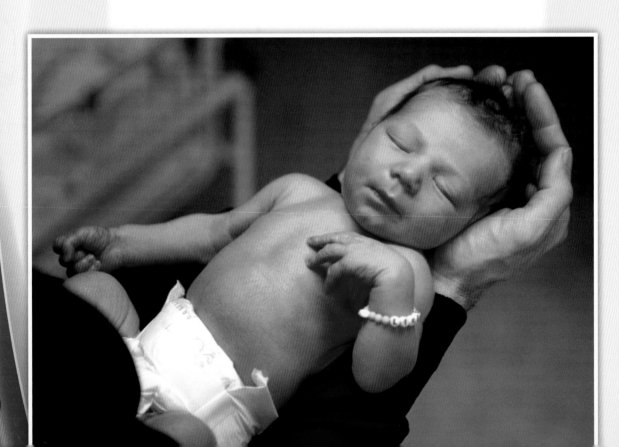

◄This boy meets his new sister for the first time.

It is fun to meet a new brother or sister for the first time. Many **hospitals** allow older brothers and sisters to visit their mom and the new baby. Grandparents and adult friends may visit, too.

▶ Taking care of a new baby may make your dad tired.

Babies sleep for two or three hours at a time during the day and night. Then they wake up to eat. That means parents are up in the night, too, so they may be very tired.

Babies fuss. Sometimes they cry so loudly they wake up the whole family. It takes a lot of work to keep a baby clean and happy.

◄ Babies need to be changed often.

What If I Feel Left Out?

People like to visit new babies. Grandparents, aunts, uncles, and friends smile and **coo** at the baby. They haven't forgotten the older brother or sister, but it may feel that way.

▶ Everyone wants to see the new baby.

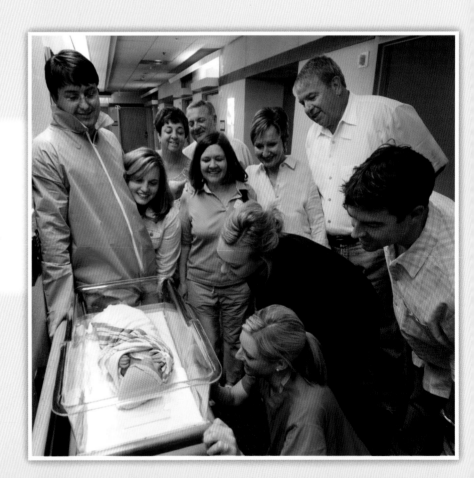

People may give the baby gifts. Sometimes they remember to bring gifts for the big brother or sister, too. But if they don't, older children may feel left out.

▲Sometimes new babies get presents.

▲Older children sometimes feel left out when a new baby joins the family.

Babies need help because they cannot do anything for themselves. Parents must feed, clean, and calm the baby. Sometimes parents forget that you want help, too. You should ask for help when you need it.

◄ Fussing
and crying is
not the best
way to get
help.

Parents want to spend time with each
of their children. It's important to tell
your family if you are feeling left out.
Tell parents what you want and need
from them.

Sharing Your Mom and Dad

One of the hardest things about having a new sister or brother is sharing family time with the baby. At first, the baby's needs must come first. Sometimes, your parents will have to stop paying attention to you in order to take care of the baby.

▶ Sharing your parents with the new baby can be very hard.

▲You may enjoy sitting with your mom while she feeds the baby.

One way to spend time with your parents is to help take care of the baby. You can pick up toys, fold laundry, and help with meals like you did before the baby was born. Your parents will be pleased to have your help.

19

Sharing Your Things

At first, babies are too little to play with toys. But babies grow quickly. As they get older, they may want to play with your toys. You can set aside some toys to share with the baby.

▲ This girl shares a toy with her new sister.

▲ Some of your things are too small for a new baby to play with.

You don't need to share everything with the baby. Put your special things up high or in a drawer. Babies can get hurt if they play with sharp things. They should not put small or dirty things in their mouths.

◄ Getting angry at the baby never helps.

Some children feel angry when a baby brother or sister rips a drawing or grabs a toy. The baby is too little to understand that it is wrong to take someone else's things. Be kind and **gentle** with the baby. Then talk to your parents about it.

Adults can help you find a way to keep your special things safe. Maybe you can put things on a shelf out of the baby's reach. Maybe you can use a drawer or closet to keep your things safe.

▼Crawling babies get into everything.

23

A Special Job

Being a big brother or sister is a special job. You can help teach your baby brother or sister how to talk. Reading to babies helps them learn about the world around them. As babies get older, they copy what their older brothers and sisters do.

▲Older brothers and sisters can help give the baby a bath.

▼ Babies laugh when brothers and sisters do funny things.

Many children like making their little sisters and brothers laugh by making faces, dancing, or playing peek-a-boo. As babies get older, they join in the fun. Sometimes they act silly so that their older brothers and sisters will laugh at them.

Talk to an Adult

◄ It's important to let your parents know how you are feeling.

Your parents want you to be happy. Tell your parents if you are feeling left out or angry. Parents do not stop loving an older child just because they have a new baby. Parents love all their children.

It helps to talk to friends. Some children talk to their grandparents about their feelings. Others may tell a teacher. Talking about your feelings is always a good thing to do.

◄ Some children enjoy talking to a grandparent.

27

▲This baby has many older brothers and sisters. Not many families grow this big.

Having a new brother or sister is different for everyone. Each new brother or sister is special.

Many sisters and brothers become best friends. They share good times and hard times. They help each other as they grow up together.

▲Many brothers and sisters enjoy spending time together.

Glossary

adopt bring a child born to other parents into your family

coo make a soft noise

gentle kind and understanding

hospital place where ill or injured people find help. It is also the place where babies are born.

newborn baby who has just been born

pregnant expecting a baby

Find Out More

Books to Read

Hughes, Monica. *First Brother or Sister*. Chicago: Raintree, 2004.

Lasky, Kathryn. *Love That Baby!: A Book About Babies for New Brothers, Sisters, Cousins and Friends*. Cambridge, MA: Candlewick Press, 2004.

Powell, Jillian. *A New Baby*. North Mankato, MN: Smart Apple Media, 2007.

Website

• Kidshealth.org
(http://kidshealth.org/kid/feeling/home_family/new_baby.html)
is a Website that can help big brothers and sisters welcome a new baby.

Index